AF269749

LIGHTNING BOLT BOOKS™

Hardworking Military Engineering Vehicles

Brianna Kaiser

Lerner Publications ◆ Minneapolis

Lerner Publications Company
An imprint of Lerner Publishing Group, Inc.
241 First Avenue North
Minneapolis, MN 55401 USA

For reading levels and more information, look up this title at www.lernerbooks.com.

Main body text set in Billy Infant Regular. Typeface provided by SparkType.

Editor: Nicole Berglund **Photo Editor:** Nicole Berglund

Library of Congress Cataloging-in-Publication Data

Names: Kaiser, Brianna, 1996- author.
Title: Hardworking military engineering vehicles / Brianna Kaiser.
Description: Minneapolis : Lerner Publications, [2024] | Series: Lightning bolt books ® - mighty military vehicles | Includes bibliographical references and index. | Audience: Ages 6-9 | Audience: Grades 2-3 | Summary: "The military uses many kinds of engineering vehicles to move and build. From bulldozers to dump trucks, readers will enjoy exploring the technology inside these machines"— Provided by publisher.
Identifiers: LCCN 2023036360 (print) | LCCN 2023036361 (ebook) | ISBN 9798765626139 (library binding) | ISBN 9798765628973 (paperback) | ISBN 9798765635209 (epub)
Subjects: LCSH: Vehicles, Military—Juvenile literature. | Combat engineer vehicles—Juvenile literature.
Classification: LCC UG390 .K35 2024 (print) | LCC UG390 (ebook) | DDC 623.7409—dc23/eng/20230803

LC record available at https://lccn.loc.gov/2023036360
LC ebook record available at https://lccn.loc.gov/2023036361

Manufactured in the United States of America
1-1009905-51947-10/25/2023

Table of Contents

Making a Road

A big vehicle crosses a small river. Then it moves over rough, dry ground.

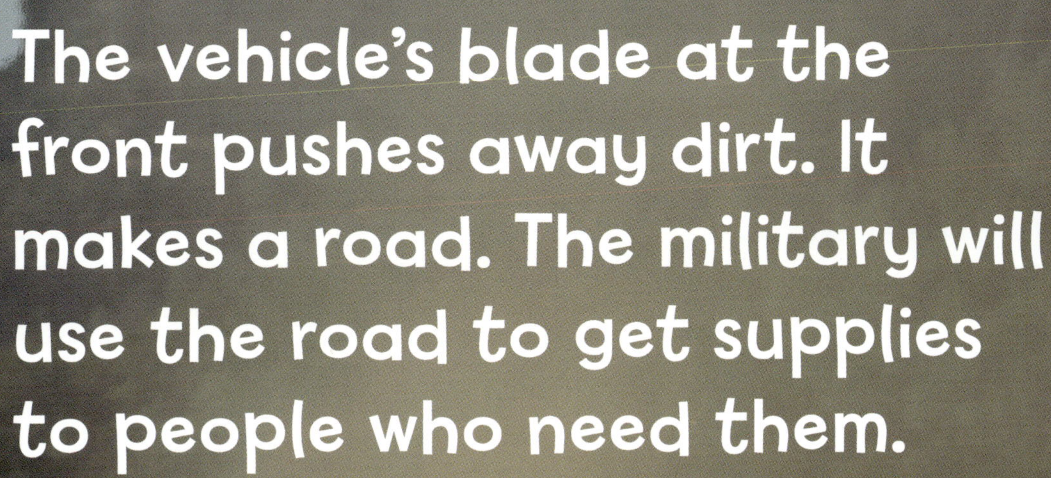

The vehicle's blade at the front pushes away dirt. It makes a road. The military will use the road to get supplies to people who need them.

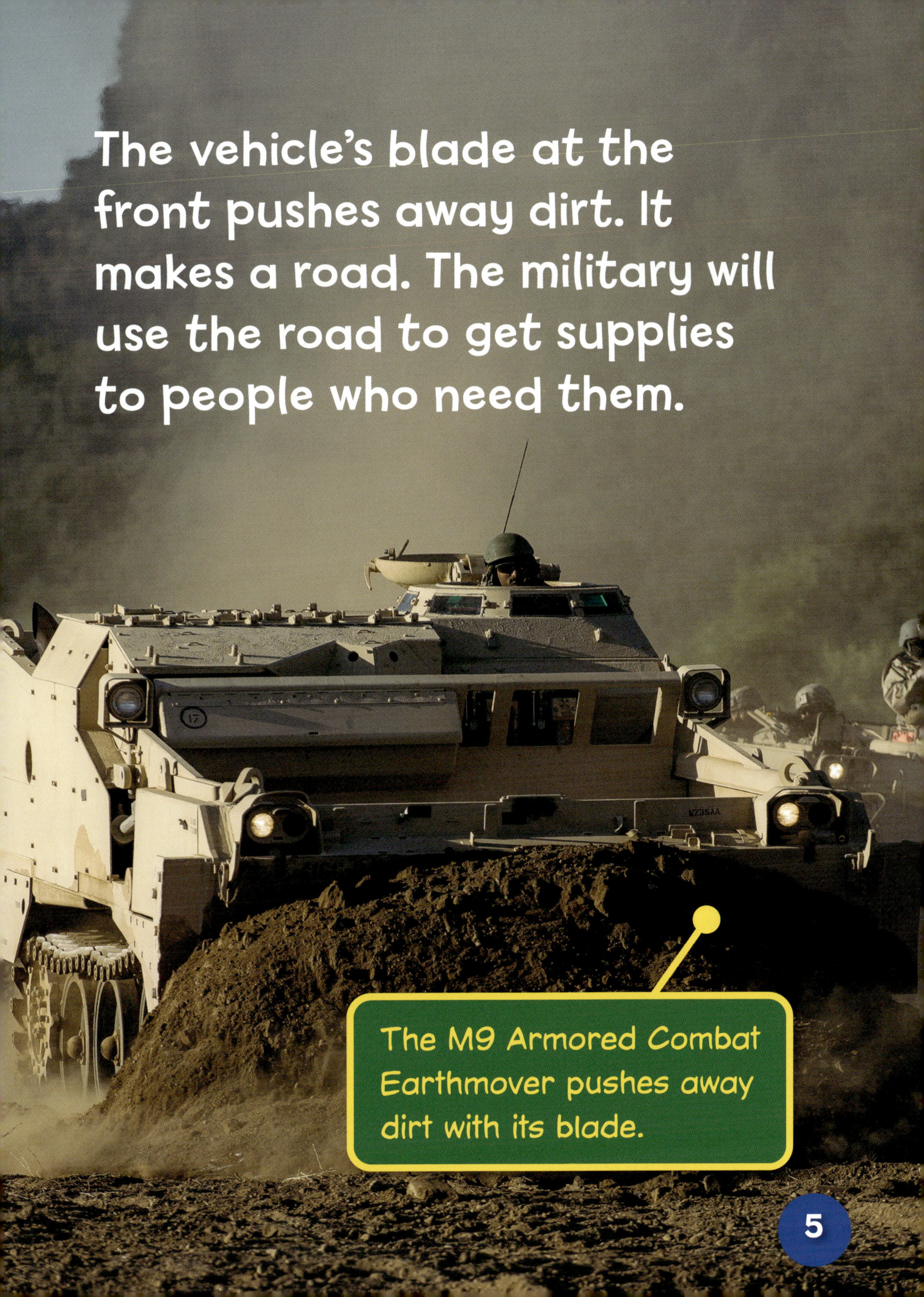

The M9 Armored Combat Earthmover pushes away dirt with its blade.

Militaries around the world use military engineering vehicles. These vehicles do many jobs. Engineers use science and math to plan and build things.

These vehicles come in lots of sizes and have different **parts.** Bulldozers, cranes, and dump trucks are types of military engineering vehicles.

Vehicles transporting supplies

Many Parts

All military engineering vehicles have powerful engines. The engines turn fuel into energy. This energy makes the vehicles work.

The vehicles also have tires or tracks. Tires and tracks are built strong. They can drive over any kind of land.

Soldiers sit inside the vehicles
while they control them.
Some vehicles can fit only one
person. Other vehicles can fit
more people.

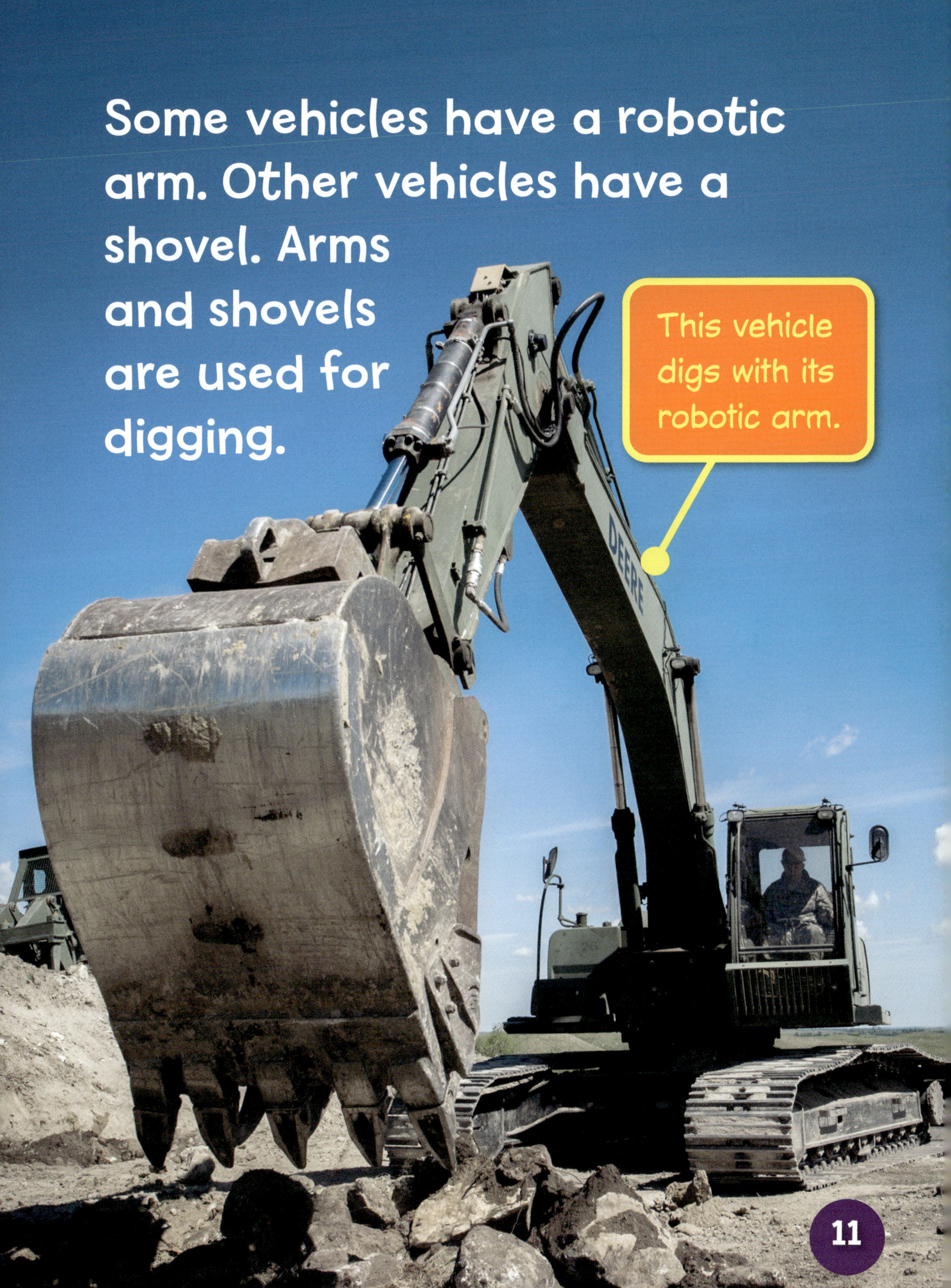

Some vehicles have a robotic arm. Other vehicles have a shovel. Arms and shovels are used for digging.

Blades can push away dirt and rock. Militaries use vehicles with blades to clear paths or areas for building.

A pathway cleared by a blade

After clearing an area, soldiers drive a vehicle that has special rollers. The rollers clear and smooth the ground.

Sometimes militaries need to move heavy objects. They can use a crane to lift the objects.

They can also use a vehicle with a winch. Winches lift and carry other vehicles.

Jobs and More

Militaries use engineering vehicles to solve problems. They can break down old buildings to make room for new ones.

The vehicles can also clear paths. This helps people reach food and water more easily. It also helps other military vehicles move from place to place.

Sometimes soldiers travel long distances. They use the vehicles to move from one area to another.

Engineers are always working on making military engineering vehicles better. How would you use one of the vehicles?

Vehicle Diagram

Hercules M88A2

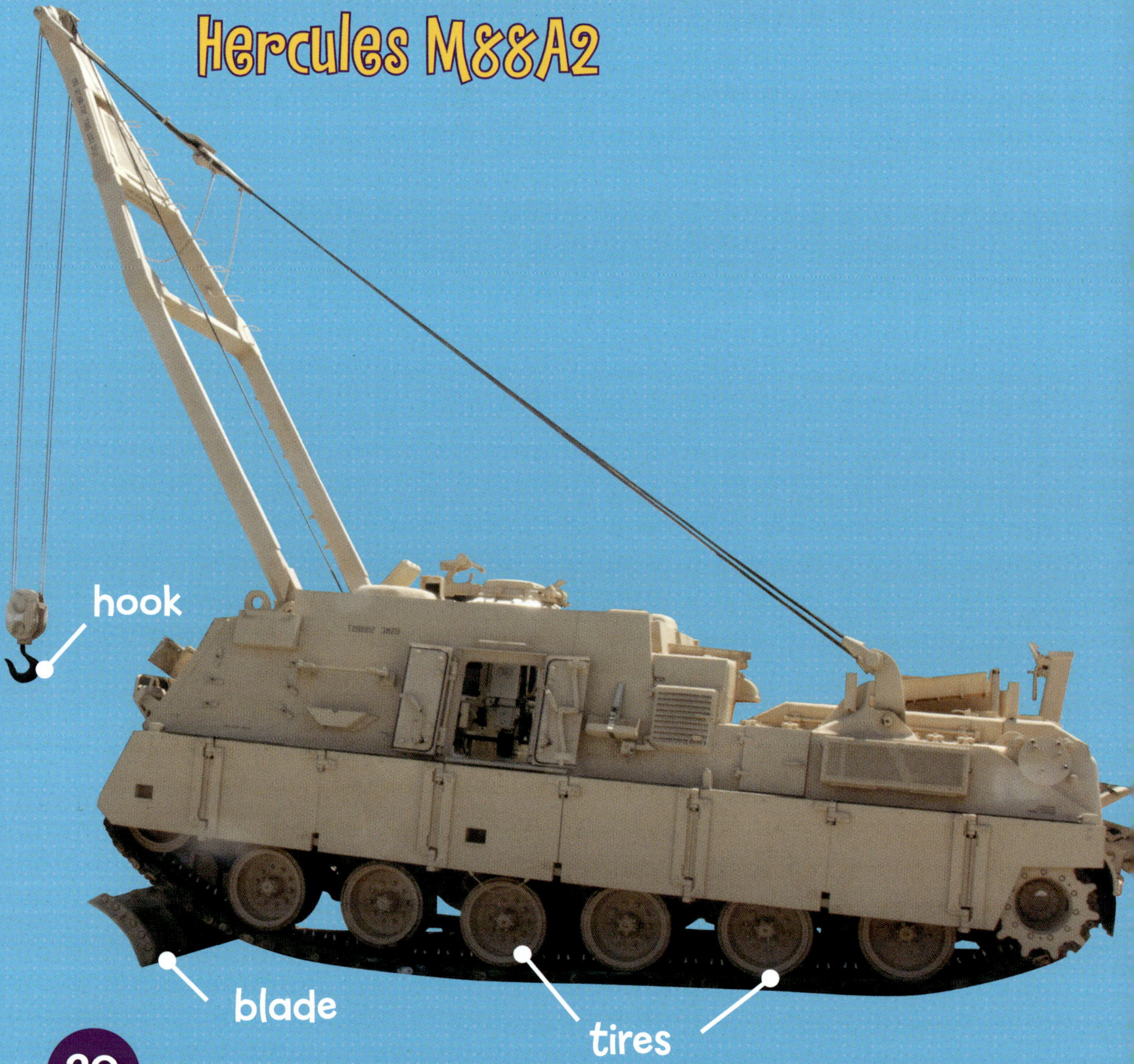

Fun Facts

- An engineer designs and builds things. Military engineers are called combat engineers.

- Bulldozers, cranes, and dump trucks are also used by construction workers.

- The M3 Amphibious Rig carries military vehicles over deep water.

Glossary

arm: a vehicle part used for digging

blade: a vehicle part used for pushing things away

crane: a vehicle that lifts things

engine: a machine that uses fuel to make a vehicle work

engineering: the use of science and math to plan and build things

roller: a vehicle part used for clearing and smoothing ground

winch: a vehicle part that lifts or carries other vehicles

Learn More

Ducksters: United States Armed Forces
https://www.ducksters.com/history/us
_government/united_states_armed_forces.php

Kaiser, Brianna. *Look Inside a Bulldozer: How It Works.* Minneapolis: Lerner Publications, 2024.

Kiddle: Military Engineering Facts for Kids
https://kids.kiddle.co/Military_engineering

Miller, Marie-Therese. *Land and Water Combat Vehicles.* Minneapolis: Lerner Publications, 2025.

National Geographic Kids: All about Engineering and Technology
https://www.natgeokids.com/uk/discover/science
/general-science/all-about-engineering-and
-technology/

Ringstad, Arnold. *The Military Vehicles Encyclopedia.* Minneapolis: Abdo, 2024.

Index

Photo Acknowledgments

Image credits: Photo by Cpl. Michael Dye, II Marine Expeditionary Force, p. 4; U.S. Army Reserve photo by Master Sgt. Michel Sauret, p. 5; U.S. Navy photo by Mass Communication Specialist 2nd Class Brent Pyfrom, p. 6; US Army National Guard Photo/Sgt. Ian M. Kummer, p. 7; U.S. Army photo/Pfc. Denae Davis, p. 8; U.S. Air National Guard photo by Tech. Sgt. Michael Matkin, p. 9; U.S. Army photo by Sgt. 1st Class Matthew Keeler, p. 10; Photo by Sgt. Brett Miller, North Dakota National Guard Public Affairs, p. 11; Photo by Lance Cpl. Chris Garcia, II Marine Expeditionary Force, p. 12; Photo by Zachary Mott, 88th Readiness Division, p. 13; U.S. Navy photo by Mass Communication Specialist 3rd Class Jacob Estes, p. 14; U.S. Army National Guard photo by Spc. Iain Jaramillo, p. 15; U.S. Army Photo by Scott T. Sturkol, Public Affairs Office, Fort McCoy, Wis., p. 16; New York Army National Guard photo by Sgt. Michael Davis, p. 17; U.S. Army Photo by Spc. Jamie Sharer, 703rd BSB, 4th IBCT, 3rd ID, p. 18; U.S. Navy photo by Mass Communication Specialist 3rd Class Justin Whitley, p. 19; Photo by Keith Hayes, Marine Corps Logistics Base Barstow, p. 20.

Cover: Photo by Staff Sgt. Coltin Heller, 109th Mobile Public Affairs Detachment.